FACET fb BOOKS

BIBLICAL SERIES – 14

John Reumann, General Editor

A Primer of Old Testament Text Criticism

by D. R. AP-THOMAS

FORTRESS PRESS PHILADELPHIA

A Primer of Old Testament Text Criticism was first published by the Epworth Press (Edgar C. Barton), London, 1947. The second, revised edition, here reprinted, was published by Basil Blackwell, Oxford, 1964, © Basil Blackwell 1965.

Library of Congress Catalog Card Number 66-21731

3398F66 Printed in U.S.A. UB3029

Introduction

STUDY of the Old Testament in general and of its Hebrew text in particular has come into greater prominence in recent years. There are a number of reasons for this—a generation of able teachers, some exciting archeological discoveries, the growth of interest in Near Eastern studies and in biblical theology, the realization (as during the Nazi period) that what does violence to the Old Testament and Hebraic studies ultimately threatens the Christian faith itself, and a renewed understanding within the Christian churches of the Old Testament as the Word of God.

This interest in the Old Testament has particularly taken the form of deepened study of the text. New appreciations of Hebrew poetry, insights from related languages like Ugaritic (its importance increasingly apparent in the last thirty-five years), and the recovery of ancient Hebrew manuscripts from caves at Qumran and neighboring areas of the Judean desert in both Jordan and Israel have been responsible. Even for laymen and pastors who know no Hebrew, the finds from the Dead Sea region have focused attention on the text and on the need for possible revisions in our English translations. One may say that just as the Greek papyrus discoveries in the late nineteenth century caused a tremendous popular interest in the text and language of the New Testament, so the Qumran manuscripts and fragments have created a somewhat comparable interest in the Old Testament in recent years.

But study of the Old Testament text is no easy matter. To the layman, textual criticism has a forbidding sound. To student or pastor who knows a bit of Hebrew the subject is awesome in its complexity, since thorough knowledge not only of Hebrew but also of a number of cognate languages, plus awareness of the history of textual transmission, and mastery of the principles of the science and art of text criticism are involved.

Technical as the topic may be, however, its very importance almost compels one to learn more about the Old Testament writings. In the face of further discoveries of intertestamental documents, how, we may ask, have different groups defined the canon? In what languages was the Old Testament written, and how did the traditional Hebrew text evolve? What light do the translations made into Greek and other languages in ancient times shed on our Hebrew text? (The area of the Greek versions alone bids to be revolutionized by recent manuscript discoveries in Palestine.) What debts do we legitimately owe to the generations of Jewish scholars called "Masoretes" who fixed and handed on the Old Testament Hebrew text, and what errors can be spotted in their text, now that we have evidence from the Dead Sea Scrolls which vaults us back behind the time when the Masoretes worked?

These and similar questions D. R. Ap-Thomas, of the faculty of University College, Bangor, Wales, undertakes to answer in this Facet Book. There are, of course, many technical monographs and articles in the periodical literature on various aspects of Old Testament text criticism. Handbooks treat the topic in detail for seminary and university students who read Hebrew. The present little volume seeks to provide a "primer" or first introduction for students who are just learning Hebrew and for laymen who, even though they are without any introduction to the Hebrew language, want to know something about the text of the Old Testament. Five of the six chapters have been drawn up with virtually no use of the Hebrew alphabet, so that all readers can readily follow this material. The final chapter, on problems and errors in the Hebrew text, can scarcely be presented without citing some examples in Hebrew, for even transliteration will not always make clear the point involved. Hence chapter six employs the Hebrew alphabet in giving examples, but it is hoped that even here readers without previous knowledge of this alphabet will be able to follow the general contentions, and perhaps see the issues involved from the Hebrew words themselves. The author does not refrain from discussing technical items, but his aim in the book is, as he phrased it in the first edition, "to pave more smoothly the path of the beginner in the study of God's Word in the Old Testament."

Dafydd Rhys Ap-Thomas is the seventh son of a Welsh Congregational minister. He holds the degrees of B.A. (Wales), B.D. (London), and M.A. (Oxon.), having studied Semitics under Edward Robertson at University College, Bangor, 1930–34, and theology at Mansfield College, Oxford, 1934–37. While at Oxford he specialized in Old Testament under H. Wheeler Robinson and G. A. Cooke. In the thirties, prior to World War II, he was also able to pursue advanced work in the Semitics field in Germany, under Johannes Hempel at Berlin, where he also heard lectures by Alfred Bertholet, Ernst Sellin, E. Ebeling, R. Hartmann, and H. H. Schaeder. Broader interests in early church history also led him to attend the lectures of Hans Lietzmann, who was warden of the hostel where he lived.

Mr. Ap-Thomas returned to Bangor in his native Wales in 1938, where he served as assistant to Professor H. H. Rowley. He is today still teaching at the University College there, holding the title of Senior Lecturer in Hebrew and Biblical Studies. From 1961 to 1964 he occupied the post of Dean of Divinity of the (federal) University of Wales. He is well-known as Domestic Secretary (since 1960) of the British Society for Old Testament Study. In the fall of 1965 he was Visiting Professor in the Department of Near Eastern Studies at the University of Toronto, in Canada.

In addition to papers at international congresses and articles in a number of learned journals, Mr. Ap-Thomas has contributed articles to the revised one-volume Hastings' *Dictionary of the Bible* (1963), the G. W. Thatcher Memorial Volume (ed. E. B. MacLaurin), and the volume edited by D. Winton Thomas for the Society for Old Testament Study, *Archaeology and Old Testament Study* (both forthcoming). As a translator, he has put into English two chapters in *The Old Testament and Modern Study* (ed. H. H. Rowley, 1951) and the volume *The Laws in the Pentateuch and Other Essays* by the German scholar Martin Noth. In addition, he was responsible for the translation from the Norwegian of Sigmund Mowinckel's final work on the Psalter, *The Psalms in Israel's Worship* (2 vols., 1962).

The Rev. Mr. Ap-Thomas served as pastor of a small church in Wales for ten years and has found time over the years to do considerable preaching and radio broadcasting. He has spent two seasons excavating in Palestine with the British School of Archaeology in Jerusalem.

This Facet Books edition reproduces the second, revised British edition which made a number of changes in and additions to the first edition (1947). A few departures from the normal style of Facet Books have been allowed, in order to follow exactly the author's mode of presentation in this technical area. However, about a dozen minor misprints and errors in the second British edition have been corrected. I wish to thank the Rev. Foster R. McCurley, Jr., S.T.M., instructor in Hebrew at the Lutheran Theological Seminary, Philadelphia, for going over the galley proofs of the British edition and making a number of such suggestions. The author has noted still others and has approved all the changes.

The books and articles cited by their short titles in this Introduction and in the book itself are listed with full bibliographical data at the end, under the heading "For Further Reading."

JOHN REUMANN

Lutheran Theological Seminary
Philadelphia August, 1965

Contents

Foreword

THIS book is intended for students beginning the critical study of Hebrew texts. It has therefore been kept in as elementary a form as possible—indeed, except in the last chapter, no knowledge at all of Hebrew is required of the reader.

A preliminary study of these six chapters should help to avoid that Scylla and Charybdis so familiar to every teacher: on the one hand, the loss of precious time entailed if he first explains the whole paraphernalia of text criticism during class, or on the other, the bewilderment of the student suddenly confronted with the presuppositions and technical terms which are the tools of his new craft.

The aim throughout has been usefulness, not novelty. Consequently, I have borrowed freely where I profitably could, though never, it is hoped, without the exercise of independent judgment. The Introductions of Ginsburg, Eissfeldt, and Pfeiffer have helped me considerably in different fields, and I gladly acknowledge my debt to them.

This second edition has been completely re-set, but, with the exception of a short addition dealing with the Dead Sea Scrolls, the temptation to expand has been resisted, the better to preserve the aim of the book as expressed above. The thanks of myself and my readers are due to the numerous friends who not only have been pressing for a re-issue of this Primer but in many cases have sent corrections and suggestions which I have been glad to incorporate; I would mention especially the Revs. W. A. Davies, late of New College, London, and E. R. Rowlands of University College, Cardiff.

1

THE CANON OF THE OLD TESTAMENT

BEFORE we undertake to study the text of the Old Testament, it would be as well to have some idea as to how the Old Testament came to consist of just so many books in just such an order, i.e. how the *canon* of the Old Testament came to be formed.

The word *canon* meant originally a *reed*, then it meant a *measuring rod* or *rule*, then a *rule* or *regulation*, then a *standard* or an *inventory*. There are other variations of meaning, but it is these last two which explain the meaning for our present purpose: the canon of the Old Testament is the *standard list of its contents*.

There are two forms of the Old Testament which concern us: (*a*) that of the Jews of Palestine, and (*b*) that of the Jews of Alexandria in Egypt. The difference between them is one of both order and extent. There is an excess of the Alexandrian over the Palestinian canon which forms the literature known to us as the Apocrypha, since the Protestant Christian Church has adopted the limits of the shorter Palestinian, or Hebrew, canon, although it curiously enough follows the Alexandrian, or Greek, order of books.

The difference in the order of books is partly due to the fact that they are grouped on different principles. In Palestine the books fall into three groups (Law,

Prophets, Writings) corresponding to their respective dates of acceptance as Scripture, or the degree of authority ascribed to them. In Egypt, on the other hand, the arrangement in four groups (Law, History, Poetry, Prophecy) is more strictly in accordance with subject matter (e.g. Chronicles put after Kings), setting (e.g. Ruth put after Judges), or reputed authorship (e.g. Lamentations put after Jeremiah). It should be noted that the examples cited above all involve changing the *group* in which the first book stands. Variation in the *order* of the books within any group is not significant; it occurs frequently in different manuscripts. The reason for this is that until the more comprehensive book-form of manuscript was adopted, each book had to be written on a separate roll for practical reasons of handling, and consequently it would have no fixed place *vis-à-vis* its fellows unless its subject matter demanded it.

The easiest way to see the difference between the two forms of the Old Testament current in ancient times is to have them set out in parallel columns as below:

Palestinian Canon[1]	*Alexandrian Canon*[2]
I. LAW (Torah)	I. LAW
Genesis[3]	Genesis[3]
Exodus	Exodus
Leviticus	Leviticus
Numbers	Numbers
Deuteronomy	Deuteronomy

[1] The order of books as given in Kittel's *Biblia Hebraica*, Third Edition, is followed here; the order within Groups II and III varies in ancient authorities.

[2] The list and order given in Rahlf's *Septuaginta* are followed here. Books not found in the Palestinian canon (i.e. Apocrypha) are enclosed

Palestinian Canon	*Alexandrian Canon*
II. PROPHETS (Nebiim)	II. HISTORY
(*a*) Former Prophets	
Joshua	Joshua
Judges	Judges
(*See Group III*)	Ruth
Samuel (1 and 2)[1]	1 Samuel (1 Kingdoms)
	2 Samuel (2 Kingdoms)
Kings (1 and 2)[1]	1 Kings (3 Kingdoms)
	2 Kings (4 Kingdoms)
(*See Group III*)	1 Chronicles
	2 Chronicles
	[1 Esdras]
(*See Group III*)	Ezra-Nehemiah (2 Esdras)
(*See Group III*)	Esther
	[Judith]
	[Tobit]
	[1 Maccabees]
	[2 Maccabees]
	[3 Maccabees]
	[4 Maccabees]
(*b*) Latter Prophets	(*See Group IV*)
Isaiah	
Jeremiah	
Ezekiel	
'The Twelve'[2]	
III. WRITINGS (Kethubim)	III. POETRY
Psalms	Psalms
	[Odes[3]]
Job	Proverbs

[1] This book is not bisected in Hebrew MSS.

[2] The twelve 'Minor Prophets' were anciently regarded as one book. They are always the same twelve (Hosea, Joel, Amos, Obadiah, Jonah, Micah, Nahum, Habakkuk, Zephaniah, Haggai, Zechariah, Malachi), but their order varies slightly in ancient MSS.

[3] These are poetical pieces gathered from other parts of the Greek Bible for ecclesiastical convenience.

---

in square brackets. Variation in the number of apocryphal books included and the order within Groups II–IV is common in ancient authorities.

[3] The Hebrew names of books in the Pentateuch (i.e. Group I) consist of the first significant word in the books, so also Canticles and Lamentations; for the remainder, either the subject matter or the reputed author's name supplies the title. The English names are taken from the Greek via the Latin Vulgate, except for Samuel, Kings, Ezra and Nehemiah. Divergent Greek names are put in round brackets.

Palestinian Canon	*Alexandrian Canon*
Proverbs	Ecclesiastes
Ruth	(*See Group II*)
Canticles (Song of Solomon)	Canticles
Ecclesiastes	Job
	[Wisdom (Wisdom of Solomon)]
	[Ecclesiasticus (Wisdom of Sirach)]
	[Psalms of Solomon]
Lamentations	(*See Group IV*)
Esther	(*See Group II*)
Daniel	(*See Group IV*)
Ezra-Nehemiah[1]	(*See Group II*)
Chronicles (1 and 2)[2]	(*See Group II*)
(*See Group IIb*)	IV. PROPHECY
	'The Twelve'[3]
	Isaiah
	Jeremiah
	[Baruch]
(*See Group III*)	Lamentations
	[Epistle of Jeremy]
	Ezekiel
	[Susannah]
(*See Group III*)	Daniel
	[Bel and the Dragon]

The books of the Bible did not start as 'Scripture'. Canonization was the result of a gradual process of selection and rejection. It was the recognition of the *status quo* rather than an innovation, though no doubt the final closure to the Palestinian canon was applied as a defence against unorthodox books. The Alexandrian canon always lagged behind the Palestinian, and never became a definitive list, except in the first group (the Law), so that, strictly speaking, it is incorrect—though convenient—to speak of an 'Alexandrian canon'.

We know of no definite conciliar acts of canonization apart from the report that the Rabbis, who gathered

[1] One book in Hebrew.
[2] See footnote [1], p. 3.
[3] See footnote [2], p. 3.

themselves into a kind of legislative body at Jamnia (Jabneh) on the Palestine coast after the fall of Jerusalem, fixed the ultimate limits of the Hebrew canon towards the end of the first century A.D. (though the canonicity of Esther, Ecclesiastes and Canticles was a controversial topic for another generation). It is clear that at any rate the first two groups of the Palestinian canon were virtually closed many years earlier than this. Eissfeldt would give the year of Ezra's promulgation of the Law as the year in which the Pentateuch, in all essentials as it is now, was effectively canonized (Nehemiah viii. 1 ff.). This was 458 B.C. according to some, including Eissfeldt, though most scholars incline to the date 397. Some special importance must have attached itself to the Pentateuch before the middle of the third century at all events, because it was clearly 'Scripture' to the Alexandrians when they translated it into Greek at that period. As we have said, the latter never attributed the same sanctity to the subsequent groups, and we find those interspersed with apocryphal books, but the Law never. The Samaritans, who broke off relations with the Jews possibly in Nehemiah's time (*c.* 434 B.C.), never recognized any canon but that of the Law. This suggests that no other books had then acquired the peculiar sanctity of the Pentateuch.

This does not mean that the 'Former Prophets' were not in existence before the Pentateuch was canonized —indeed, they may once have formed part of it as a continuous historical work—but they never attained the same importance as the Law, though they always follow it immediately and in the same order in both canons. They and the 'Latter Prophets'—a descriptive distinction which cannot be traced earlier than the eighth century A.D.—were a fixed corpus of Scripture by 200 B.C. at the latest, for Ben Sira (Ecclesiasticus xlvi. 1–xlix. 12) refers to them all *c.* 190 B.C. as if well established. It should be noted too that Daniel, almost certainly composed *c.* 164 B.C., finds no place in the Hebrew Prophetic group, as it probably would have done had the door not been already closed. This does not of course mean that additions of one sort and another were not made to books already in, though this is not very likely.

The third division of the Hebrew canon is the most uncertain of all in its dates. Ben Sira's grandson (*c.* 117 B.C.) knows of a group of writings which he calls variously 'the others who followed after them (*sc.* after the Law and the Prophets)', 'the rest of the books', and 'the other books of our fathers'; but he gives no clue as to the titles comprised. Luke xxiv. 44 refers to this group under the name 'Psalms', naming the whole section after the first item in it, which again does not help; and it is not until the end of the first century A.D. that Josephus and 2 (4) Esdras, by numbering the total of Old Testament books recognized, make it certain that the Writings ('Hagiographa') that we know were all included.

2

LANGUAGE, SCRIPT, AND WRITING MATERIALS

If we are really to understand the Old Testament, we must have some practical equipment for the task. Obviously the first requirement is to be able to understand the real meaning of this monument to the life of a people whose religion has influenced the course of world history. This understanding cannot be fully attained without a knowledge of the language of the Old Testament.

The Old Testament is written mostly in Hebrew; but Ezra iv. 8–vi. 18 and vii. 12–26 are in Aramaic, as is Daniel ii. 4–vii. 28. The single verse Jeremiah x. 11 is also in Aramaic, and a few words in this language occur here and there in the Old Testament. Aramaic and Hebrew are nearly related, though a knowledge of Aramaic was not usual among the ordinary Israelites before the Exile (see 2 Kings xviii. 26). According to Deuteronomy xxvi. 5, the ancestors of Israel were Aramaeans, and so naturally would speak Aramaic. If this is true, it seems most likely that they dropped their Aramaic on entering Canaan, and adopted the language of the land, viz. the language we call 'Hebrew' (see M. Noth, *The History of Israel*, second edition, p. 83). Hebrew was a local dialect of Canaanite (W. F.

Albright, *From the Stone Age to Christianity*, p. 182); it was very similar to Moabite as found on the 'Moabite Stone' (*c.* 840 B.C.) (see S. R. Driver, *Notes on the Book of Samuel*, second edition, pp. lxxxiv ff.), and to Ammonite and Edomite.

Gradually, after their return from the Babylonian Exile, the Jews lost their Hebrew tongue and spoke Aramaic. That the returning exiles still spoke Hebrew is proved by the writings of Haggai and Zechariah. Nehemiah (*c.* 444 B.C.) speaks of the decay of the language however (Nehemiah xiii. 24), and eventually Hebrew became a 'dead language', used only in connection with religious affairs. The language which took its place was Aramaic—though this can hardly have been the 'speech of Ashdod' against which Nehemiah inveighed (*ibid.*). The actual change over was not abrupt, but gradual, and it must have been well on its way by the middle of the second century B.C., since, as was noted above, part of Daniel is written in Aramaic.

In time, the knowledge of Hebrew became so faint that after the reading of the Hebrew Scriptures in the synagogue, a vernacular Aramaic paraphrase was given so that the people could understand what had been read. These, sometimes loose, translations ('Targumim') attained quite an authoritative position, and some of them have survived in writing. In their present form they may be tentatively dated about the fifth century A.D. (see below, pp. 25ff).

Old Testament writing also had a varied history. The oldest writing native to Palestine proper seems to be the old Phoenician alphabet (Albright, *F.S.A.C.*, second edition, p. 75). Four inscriptions earlier than 900 B.C., written with these ancient characters, have been discovered on Israelite sites, and the earliest Old Testament passages may have been written in this script originally. The most ancient manuscript of the whole Old Testament extant, A.D. 1008–10 is not written in this old script, however, but in a different form called 'square Hebrew' or 'Assyrian script'. This shows a marked change from the old type, and it is a modification of the characters used for Aramaic. A convenient table for comparing these scripts may be seen at the beginning of Gesenius-Kautzsch, *Hebrew Grammar* (tr. Cowley), or in D. Diringer, *The Story of Aleph Beth*, pl. 2, 3.

This change-over in writing is attested by the Talmud (Sanhedrin, 21*b*, Soncino edn. I. 119), where we read: 'Originally the law was given to Israel in the *Hebrew* character and in the sacred tongue: it was given again to them in the days of Ezra in the *Assyrian* [i.e. square] character and in the Aramaic tongue. Israel chose for themselves the Assyrian character and the sacred tongue.' It would naturally be gathered from the above statement that the change-over took place in the time of Ezra; but this again is a case in which later development has been referred back to an earlier age. The earliest example yet discovered of Hebrew written in the square character is the name 'Tobiah' found as an inscription at 'Araq el-Emir east of Jordan. This man was probably the grandfather of Hyrcanus who lived hereabouts from 183–176 B.C. The change to the square character may have taken place soon after

200 B.C., although on coins the old letters were used even up to A.D. 135. The Samaritan Pentateuch is still written in a form of the old Phoenician script, but Matthew v. 18 proves that at least the Law portion of the Old Testament was written in the square characters when this Gospel was written, since the letter *yodh* (jot) is not the smallest letter of the old script.

It will be as well now to seek some idea of what an ancient Hebrew document looked like. Royal edicts or records might be cut in stone, like the Mesha' inscription in Moab. But, so far, these are conspicuous by their absence on Israelite soil proper. The nearest it can offer as yet is the Siloam tunnel inscription, *c.* 700 B.C. carved on the side of the aqueduct which brought water from the Virgin's Spring to the Pool of Siloam in Jerusalem. This inscription consists in its present incomplete state of just over fifty words (see Driver's *Samuel*, pp. vii ff, D. Winton Thomas, *Documents from O.T. Times*, pp. 209 ff). The Gezer 'calendar' inscription gives an example of a small inscribed tablet; but much more numerous are the pieces of broken unglazed earthenware ('potsherds' or 'ostraca') which were picked up from the street when required and had the message written in ink with a reed pen. An important collection of these has been found at Tell ed-Duweir (the Old Testament Lachish) and dating from the time of Jeremiah. But these hardly rank as literary works, in spite of their importance.

Although we must no doubt reckon with a time when parts of the Old Testament were written on nothing but ostraca—especially prophetic oracles—yet our chief attention must be paid to a different writing medium. As regards material written upon, it might be leather, vellum or papyrus, and as regards form it might be similar to a modern book (i.e. a 'codex') or in the form of a roll. Codices were probably not used before the second century A.D. by the Jews; nor was vellum (a prepared animal skin) used as early as papyrus, since the former was only invented (in Pergamum—whence it derived the other name for it, 'parchment') when the Egyptian monopolists of papyrus refused to export it—so we are told. Papyrus is the inner pith of the reed of the same name which grew abundantly in the Nile. It was squeezed flat; then these narrow thin strips were fastened together with glue, like trellis work—without the spaces between strips—thus giving a vertical writing surface on the back, but a horizontal one on the face. In the first instance, only the horizontal side was used; but an old roll might be used anew by writing on its back when papyrus was scarce or expensive. Furthermore, the original writing was sometimes sponged off and the roll used again; such a piece of papyrus is called a 'palimpsest'. By modern methods, the underlying writing can sometimes be restored, and so the work of an author which had been given up as lost has in more than one case been recovered.

The papyrus roll was usually ten to twelve inches high, but could be as long as needed, up to a practical maximum of thirty-five feet. It was manipulated by attaching a short wooden roller at each end, with part projecting as a handle. The writing was in short vertical columns a few inches wide, side by side and separated by a narrow gap; the book was read by uncovering one column, rolling it up on the other roller as reading progressed (see further in Kenyon, *Books and Readers in ancient Greece and Rome*, second edn., 1951).

3

VOCALIZATION AND STANDARDIZATION OF THE TEXT

Books were not written in ancient times for the ordinary person to read so much as for the scholar to refer to in uncertainty, or in order to preserve knowledge of a special kind in sacred or royal archives. Consequently, the absence of vowel signs in all Hebrew manuscripts before the seventh century A.D. was not a matter of great concern or inconvenience to anyone until Hebrew became a dead language. When Hebrew became less and less known, the absence of vowel signs threatened to become a serious drawback to the correct understanding, as well as to the correct pronunciation, of the Holy Writ. Several attempts to provide a system of vocalization were made. The first may be regarded as the use of the consonants ה, ו and י to mark the presence in a word of long vowels which are not diphthongal in origin. We do not know when this took place, but it seems to have been fairly early, as they are found in the Mesha' and Siloam Tunnel inscriptions. It is to be noted that, possibly due to conservatism, they are not as frequent in the Pentateuch as in later books, and the evidence of the Greek version from the third century B.C. suggests that many were inserted in the Hebrew text after that date.

After this partial attempt at vocalization, no others were successful in gaining a lasting foothold until the consonantal text had gained such sanctity in the eyes of the Jews that they would not consider any tampering with it. So both in Palestine and in Babylonia systems were adopted in which the vowel signs were written above the line of consonants; but the method which was finally triumphant was that of the Jews of the important Masoretic school in Tiberias. This is the system used for all 'pointed' (i.e. vocalized) Hebrew to-day. Under this system, Hebrew pronunciation was standardized. But transliterations into other scripts (e.g. Greek lettering) suggest that it was not the ordinary pronunciation current at the time, nor the original one, but an artificial form (at least in part) which was thought to be the most suitable for public reading (cf. the custom of 'intoning' readings amongst some religious bodies to-day). It is probable that this fixing of an artificial vocalization has also somewhat altered the grammatical structure of the language (see A. Sperber in *Hebrew Union College Annual*, XII–XIII, pp. 103–274).

Although vocalization of the consonantal text did not take place until the seventh century of the present era, and vowels have never really become an official part of the Jewish Scriptures, the consonantal text became fairly well defined at the beginning of the first century. Various recensions continued in existence, but no great changes can be dated after the activities of Rabbi Akiba round about A.D. 100, if we except the separation of words by a small space, which helped considerably in the preservation of the existing text. Rules were gradually evolved with regard to the writing, material and format, etc., of MSS. which ensured greater accuracy—or, rather, greater conformity to the exemplar—in copying. These rules are listed in such works as the *Massekheth Sepher Torah* or its enlarged form, known as *Massekheth Sopherim*—which both antedate the vowel points (see C. D. Ginsburg, *Introduction to the Hebrew Bible*, p. 451)—or the still larger treatise, *Sopherim*, from the eighth century. The very fact that such rules came into being supposes a period when scribes were less careful, and owners of MSS. felt quite free to add their own words of comment on the margin of their possessions. Manuscripts, since they are written by hand, are naturally open to alteration. The only method of perpetuating or multiplying any work was by copying. One scribe might dictate to another or to a group; or a scribe might copy direct from the MS. himself.

The original MS. of the author, i.e. a book as first written down, is called the *autograph*. No autograph exists to-day of any Old Testament or New Testament book—or, indeed, of any classical work either. The MS. which serves as the example for a copy is called the *exemplar* of the latter. If the MS. is not the immediate parent of the other, but a remoter ancestor, then it is called its *archetype*: e.g. if 'A' is the actual MS. written by the author Joel, then 'A' is the autograph of the Book of Joel. If 'B' is a copy made direct from 'A', and 'C' is a copy made from 'B', then 'A' is the exemplar of 'B', and 'B' is the exemplar of 'C'; but

'A' is only the archetype of 'C', since the text has been transmitted indirectly from 'A' to 'C', i.e. through 'B'.

A standard text of the Hebrew Bible was prepared by Aaron ben Moses ben Asher in the first half of the tenth century A.D., with vowel signs and accents. These latter were invented to mark the punctuation and stressed syllables, and to act as a musical guide in chanting. Ben Asher's text survives in two first-hand copies, one which used to be in Aleppo but is now in Jerusalem, and the other in Leningrad. A rival edition of the text was made by ben Asher's contemporary, Moses ben David ben Naphtali, but this—differing for the most part only in minor points—did not gain such favour, and is only preserved in part. It has probably affected the text of ben Asher slightly.

Until recent times, all printed Hebrew Bibles followed the text of Jacob ben Chayyim's four-volume Bible published at Venice in 1524–5 on the basis of Hebrew MSS. of the preceding two centuries. Now we have the third (or later) edition of the *Biblia Hebraica*, edited by R. Kittel, A. Alt and O. Eissfeldt, in which P. Kahle has checked the whole against the Leningrad copy of ben Asher's text mentioned above; and there is the British and Foreign Bible Society edition by N. H. Snaith.

The oldest surviving portion of the Hebrew Bible was once considered to be the Nash Papyrus, a scrap of Deuteronomy (v. 6—18 and vi. 4–5) dated in the second century A.D. by Pfeiffer, though W. F. Albright dates it 150–100 B.C. But since 1947 the whole position with regard to Hebrew MSS. of the Biblical text has been revolutionized by the discovery of at least part of the library belonging to a Jewish sect who lived a secluded, monastic life on the rocky spur now called Qumran which juts out from the Judaean hills towards the Dead Sea near its northern end. The MSS. found had been hidden in caves in the cliffs behind the settlement; they date from the beginning of the second century B.C. on into the first century A.D. There are copies of unique sectarian books and of books from the Apocrypha, but for our purpose the most important fact is that the Qumran finds have yielded at least fragments from every book of the Old Testament (except, so far, Esther). The longest Biblical texts are the two virtually complete scrolls of the book of Isaiah; but the Qumran library possessed at least seventeen MSS. of the Psalms and several copies of many other Old Testament books. (A convenient brief resumé may be found in Millar Burrows, *More Light on the Dead Sea Scrolls*, pp. 135–64).

A study of these MSS. shows, briefly, three things: (*a*) as already known, the Biblical text was preserved in many slightly different forms, of which the present Masoretic Text was one; (*b*) the general superiority of the M.T. over any other text-form is confirmed; (*c*) considerable caution is needed in emending the M.T. on the basis of the Dead Sea Scrolls' texts. An interesting feature of some of the MSS. is the very free use made of vowel letters—the vowel points were, of course, not yet in use. It is almost as if Hebrew were a foreign language to the scribe or, at least, not very familiar in written form. Perhaps familiarity with Greek script, which expresses all the vowels, had something to do with the tendency to multiply vowel letters in some cases.

Apart from the Dead Sea Scrolls only a few, fragmentary, Hebrew MSS. can be dated before the sixth century (see Kahle in *Prolegomena* to Kittel's *Biblia Hebraica*, third edition, pp. x–xi). The British Museum has a copy of the Pentateuch dated in the ninth century, and Leningrad possessed a copy of the Prophets dated A.D. 916, together with a copy of the whole Old Testament (as mentioned above, p. 9) which dates back to A.D. 1008–10. Slightly older is the copy of ben Asher's Old Testament which used to be in Aleppo, and younger, an almost complete MS. in Oxford (see F. Kenyon, *The Story of the Bible*, p. 11).

The list shows that, apart from the Dead Sea Scrolls, we have scarcely any evidence for the Hebrew text before it was standardized by Akiba in the first century, or even by ben Asher in the tenth. This is because all available MSS. which showed a divergent text were destroyed. A means of overcoming this difficulty to a certain extent is found by studying early translations of the Hebrew into other languages, especially the one into Greek, which was the earliest and in many ways the best for text-critical purposes.

4

THE ANCIENT VERSIONS

TRANSLATIONS of the Old Testament into other languages are known as *Versions*. To be valuable for text-critical purposes, they must have been translated before A.D. 500. It will readily be seen that, if the translator had a text different from ours, then his translation should show it and give a clue to his original. By translating back into Hebrew, we can often reconstruct a text—supported by the Version—which is better than the standard Masoretic Text.

The general principles underlying the use of Versions for correcting the M.T. are as follows:

(1) The *a priori* probability is that the M.T. is superior to any translation because of its more continuous tradition.

(2) The possibility must always be borne in mind that the text of the Version itself may have suffered corruption, e.g. in 1 Samuel x. 2 the M.T. has 'in the bounds of Benjamin' but the Greek has 'in the mountain of Benjamin', εν τω ορει B., which is clearly a corruption of the correct translation, εν τω οριω B.

(3) A slight variation in rendering may be due merely to a paraphrase and not to a different Hebrew text.

(4) The rendering of an unusual, or already corrupt,

Hebrew word by a word with a quite different meaning may be due to a guess on the part of the translator.

(5) A shorter text in the Version may be due to accidental or deliberate omission; and a longer text may be due to explanation or comment.

In short, every case of discrepancy between the M.T. and a Version must be decided on its merits, individually, after the main idiosyncrasies of that particular translator have been discovered. It should be borne in mind that a change in translators may be detected within many books of the Old Testament, as well as from book to book.

Greek Versions

The Septuagint (LXX)

The oldest and most important translations of the Old Testament are the Greek—in particular, that one known as the 'Translation of the Seventy'. It is usually referred to as the 'Septuagint' or, for short, the LXX. This name was given to it because of the tradition that it was the work of seventy (to be exact, seventy-two) men. The classic form of this tradition is that found in the 'Letter of Aristeas' (see in *The Apocrypha and Pseudepigrapha of the Old Testament*, edited by R. H. Charles, vol. II). This letter is a document of a rather fanciful character written *c.* 100 B.C. or a little earlier; it is a legend in growth, but it must have a kernel of truth. Briefly, the letter says that the High Priest Eleazar of Jerusalem sent down to Egypt six elders from each tribe with a copy of the Law, in order to translate it into Greek for Demetrios Phaleros, the Royal Librarian of Alexandria. This was done rather against the inclination of Eleazar at the request of the Egyptian King Ptolemy II Philadelphos (285–247 B.C.), who sent 'Andreas and Aristeas' with rich presents to ask the favour. The elders were greeted by the King, answered all his questions with marvellous wisdom, and then prepared their translation in quietude on the island of Pharos, completing their work in exactly seventy-two days. The new translation was then approved as correct by the Jewish inhabitants, the translators were loaded with gifts from the King, and returned home. Later accounts made the story still more marvellous, alleging that each translator worked separately, but all their results exactly tallied, that the translation extended over the whole Old Testament, and that it was as divinely inspired as the Hebrew original. These stories were discredited by the Jews themselves when the Christians adopted the Greek Bible as their Scripture, and the Jews returned to the Hebrew text as the only authentic text.

Some scholars think that Philadelphos and Demetrios may have had something to do with the translation, but a more certain conclusion is that the date in the middle of the third century B.C. seems reasonable for the Law. This was certainly the first to be translated, since its style, though not eliminating a variety of translators, distinguishes it from the rest of the Old Testament in Greek. But the translation was almost certainly made by Alexandrian, not Palestinian, Jews. It is possible that a Rabbinic version of the legend is more correct. This makes the translators five in number. But this figure may really be as symbolical as the other, viz. five Law books, five translators (cf. the five men to whom Ezra dictated the Bible after the Exile, 2 Esdras, xiv. 24). At all events, the inspiration for such a translation would most naturally be the decay of Hebrew learning among the Alexandrian Jews. This theory is strengthened by the popular, non-literary, character of the translation. As a part-way step to a translation, it is almost certain that portions of the Hebrew Scriptures were written down in transcription, i.e. Hebrew words in Greek letters, as in one column of Origen's Hexapla (see below), for the benefit of those who could understand Hebrew, but could not read it.

The most important part of Scripture, the Law, being translated, the next section, the Prophets, probably followed in order of popularity, rather than of writing; and by the beginning of the Christian era at the latest, the whole Old Testament was available in Greek. Ben Sira's grandson, who was in Egypt in 117 B.C. (some say 132), tells us that 'the Law itself, the Prophets, and the rest of the books' had been translated into Greek at that time; but as he does not name the 'rest' individually we cannot be certain that all books now in the Old Testament are included under this head (see pp. 4 f.).

The quality of the translation varies considerably. The Pentateuch is generally good; and the poorness of some of the other books may be due to the poor quality of the Hebrew MSS. used. The translation of the historical books is on the whole fair; Isaiah is poor;

Jeremiah is translated from a Hebrew very different from the M.T.; Ezekiel (and Samuel) show wide divergencies at points; the Minor Prophets are often unintelligible in Greek. Some books are written with slavish literalness, others (e g Job) with great freedom.

The name LXX, which really belongs to the Pentateuch alone, is now applied to the whole Old Testament in the Greek version more or less standard before the Christian era. It is therefore an entirely Jewish translation, although preserved to us solely through Christian hands (see, further, under 'Origen', below).

Aquila

Aquila was a Christian proselyte later converted to Judaism. He was born at Pontus on the Black Sea, and became a pupil of Rabbi Akiba. By his time (*c.* 125–50) the LXX had been adopted by the Christian Church, and several loose renderings in the Greek favoured the Christians, e.g. עַלְמָה (Isaiah vii. 14) rendered παρθενος (*virgin*), not νεανις (*girl*); and the addition of 'from a tree' after 'Tell it out among the nations: The Lord reigned' (Psalm xcvi. 10). Aquila aimed at a translation which would give an absolutely faithful rendering of the Hebrew. He omits the Apocrypha, which had always been part of the complete LXX, because it was not in the Hebrew canon; and in literalness of translation went so far that he produced an almost impossible jargon. Still, he must have possessed an amazing memory and industry, because he aimed at always translating the same Hebrew word by the same Greek rendering, using words from the same Greek stem for derivatives of the same Hebrew root, and expressing every word in Hebrew by one word in the Greek. This latter trait led him to reproduce the Hebrew homonym אֵת by συν (*with*), even when the Hebrew particle was only the sign of the definite accusative. These peculiarities make his translation very valuable for reconstructing the Hebrew text used by Aquila, but unfortunately only a few fragments of Kings, Isaiah and Psalms xc–ciii, are now extant (Field's *Hexapla* preserves most pieces).

Theodotion

Another convert to Judaism, and again from Asia Minor (Ephesus), Theodotion produced an edition of the Greek revised with the aid of the contemporary Hebrew text. Some put him slightly before Aquila; others in the reign of Commodus (180–92), but P. Kahle argues that his translation of the Bible is pre-Christian. The two most important features of his work are the much longer text of Job—one-sixth longer than the LXX—and the fact that his translation of Daniel is quite different from that of the LXX (not a revision of it). Theodotion's version of Daniel has superseded the LXX translation in all extant MSS. except two (the Chigi MS. 88 and the Chester Beatty Papyrus discovered in 1930). The text underlying this is not Theodotion's own, since it is quoted by several Church Fathers and, indeed, in the New Testament itself. It was probably another early Greek version of Daniel. Theodotion seems to have been popular even among the Christians, although he appears to have omitted the Apocrypha from his canon.

Symmachos

Not much is known of Symmachos, who is said to have been an Ebionite Christian. He may have made a new translation from the Hebrew, but he utilized the earlier translations of both the LXX and Theodotion—possibly to aid him in producing a sound text free from the literalisms of Aquila. He is the last of the series that took in hand the translation of the Hebrew Old Testament into Greek.

Origen

Origen lived from 186–253, and is the outstanding Christian scholar of ancient times. He made no new translation, but sought, round about A.D. 240 in Caesarea, to obtain a complete critical edition of existing Bible texts. Believing (mistakenly) that the Hebrew text of his day was incorrupt, he compared the LXX text with it and other Greek versions by placing them in parallel columns, using special marks to indicate additions and omissions. First he gave the Hebrew, then the Hebrew written in Greek letters; to the right of these were four more columns giving the renderings of Aquila, Symmachos, the LXX and Theodotion. It was from Theodotion that he most often amplified the LXX where it was short. For some books it appears that Origen had three further translations, known by the numbers *quinta, sexta, septima*; but it is from the fact that it was mostly in six columns that the work derived its name, Hexapla. Eusebius, in his *Ecclesiastical History* (vi, 16), says that Origen also prepared a four-column (*tetrapla*) edition, omitting the Hebrew and transliteration. Neither the exact form of the Hexapla, nor its material (papyrus or vellum) is known certainly; and after the Moslem conquest of Palestine in 638, this huge work completely disappeared. The scanty remains, picked out from the works of other writers, are largely to be found in Field's *Origenis Hexaplorum quae Supersunt*, 1875. A new, fuller edition is badly needed.

Origen clearly marked in his LXX text what was, and what was not, the reading he had found; but copyists tended to omit these marks. The net result was that this careless copying led to a hopelessly confused text type. But a literal translation of Origen's LXX column was made into Syriac in 616–17 by Bishop Paul of Tella, with all Origen's critical signs. Most of this work survives and has been published, partly by A. M. Ceriani, and partly by P. de Lagarde.

Lucian

Lucian was a Christian martyred in the Maximinian persecution of 309–12. He worked at Antioch and made a blend of divergent readings, which has resulted in a text that cannot be relied on, but which contains many readings, both ancient and valuable, which otherwise would have disappeared. P. Kahle, followed by A. Sperber, believes that Lucian made a new translation. P. de Lagarde tried to gather together the text of Lucian from references in Church Fathers, but his success is questionable.

Hesychios

Hesychios was a Christian martyred in the same persecution as Lucian. He was probably an Egyptian bishop. His work again was probably to revise and correct existing LXX texts. According to Jerome in one passage (*Praef. in Paralip.*, Migne xxviii. 1,324 f.), Hesychios' recension was standard for Egypt, Lucian's from Constantinople as far as Antioch, and Origen's for Palestine and Syria. C. H. Cornill has tried to isolate the readings of Hesychios for Ezekiel.

The above list sums up the Greek versions which give evidence as to the original Hebrew text. The most convenient, though not invariably accurate, edition of the main version—the LXX—is that edited by H. B. Swete, *The Old Testament in Greek* (1st ed., 1887 ff.; 4th, 1909 ff.) in three volumes; there is also a fourth volume, *Introduction to the Old Testament in Greek* (1st ed., 1900; 2nd, revised by R. R. Ottley, 1914). The edition by A. Rahlfs, *Septuaginta* (1935) has some minor 'corrections' of Rahlfs' own; it has also a useful introduction on the Greek versions. A very elaborate edition is being published in parts, and is known as *The Cambridge Septuagint*. Mention should also be made of the important Göttingen Septuagint series.

These printed editions are, of course, dependent on MSS. of the LXX, which are almost innumerable; but the really important ones are few. Foremost amongst them is a MS. preserved in the Vatican Library at Rome, and so called the *Codex Vaticanus*, or *Codex B*. (This latter classification was begun by J. J.

Wettstein in 1751, and lists MSS. written in capitals (*uncials*) by a capital letter, but others (*cursives*) by Arabic numerals.) Codex B dates from the early fourth century, and contains all the Old Testament except Genesis i. 1–xlvi. 28, some verses in 2 Samuel, and about thirty psalms.

The *Codex Sinaiticus* (א, aleph) is also a codex of the whole Bible, and dates from the early fourth century too. Only the prophetical and poetical books are well preserved in the Old Testament.

The *Codex Alexandrinus* (A) is slightly later (early fifth century), and is not so accurate, but it lacks only a few portions of Genesis, 1 Samuel, and Psalms.

The Chester Beatty collection contains important early papyrus fragments.

Syriac Versions

The Peshitta

The 'Peshitta' (*the Simple*) translation of the Old Testament into Syriac was made by Jews—or possibly Christians—early in the Christian era (between the first and third centuries). The Pentateuch was probably the first to be translated, with the other books following later from different hands. The translation was made from the Hebrew, but has been revised according to the LXX in part. The quality varies, e.g. Chronicles is largely paraphrase. The Peshitta as a whole has not been edited thoroughly like the LXX, so that its value is not so great for critical purposes. The British and Foreign Bible Society publish a text edited by S. Lee (1823), and there is an edition published in Urmia (1852, reprint, London 1954), and another in Mosul (1887 ff., reprint, Beirut 1951). More modern editions are available for the Pentateuch, Psalms, Isaiah, Lamentations, Ezra. Peshitta studies will be much advanced when the work on a new critical edition undertaken by an international team centred on Leiden is completed.

Later Syriac Versions

None of the later translations supplanted the Peshitta, and only traces of them survive. Bishop Paul of Tella (616–17) translated Origen's LXX text, keeping all the latter's critical signs, and this remains. Its chief value is for its witness to Origen's Hexaplaric text, and it has been named the Syro-Hexaplaric Version (see p. 26).

Latin Versions

The Itala

Rome spoke Greek, so that the Bible was first translated into Latin, not in Rome, but in North Africa, in all probability. The translation was made from the Greek as needed and by anyone who so chose, according to Augustine. But it is possible that the differing MSS. of Augustine's day were really bad copies rather than separate translations. The date for the first translation attempt seems to be somewhere in the second century, but no MS. of the complete Old Testament exists now, if it ever did. Nor in all probability would it be of any great value for the Hebrew text even if discovered. This old translation is called the Old Latin

(*Vetus Latina*) or Itala. A critical edition is being issued by the Vetus Latina Institut, Beuron.

Jerome and the Vulgate

Born *c.* 346 in Dalmatia, Jerome, an accomplished Christian scholar, in fifteen years (391–405) translated the whole Old Testament into Latin direct from the Hebrew text current in his day. This was done after he had already revised the Psalter twice—the first (383) has disappeared, since the 'Roman Psalter' is probably not Hieronymian; and the 'Gallican Psalter' (386–7) was the second—as well as Job and some other books on the basis of the LXX text.

Jerome's new translation of the Psalter, though made direct from the Hebrew, never ousted his earlier 'Gallican' version, based on the LXX. The rest of his Old Testament gradually won support, but only at the expense of being contaminated by the still surviving Old Latin Bible.

The official Bible of the Roman Catholic Church to-day is the edition of Jerome's translation—known since the thirteenth century as the 'Vulgate'—published as revised and restored by a special commission in 1592. An entirely new edition was started by order of Pope Pius IX (1907); Genesis–Psalms have already appeared, and the other books will follow.

Where we have the actual translation of Jerome, it is a valuable guide to the Hebrew text current about A.D. 400, i.e. after the first great Jewish revision by Akiba, but before the final Masoretic standardization of the text and insertion of vowel points.

Aramaic Versions

The Targums (see also p. 8)

When Hebrew was no longer understood by Jewish congregations, the recitation of Targumim ('interpretations') in Aramaic followed the reading of the Hebrew Scriptures where the population was Aramaic-speaking. At first these were extempore renderings, but gradually they attained fixed written forms. They are marked by a tendency to paraphrase and to smooth out difficulties caused by both anthropomorphisms and obscurities; they occasionally add comments or tacit corrections. Targums are extant for all Old Testament books except Daniel and Ezra-Nehemiah, which are themselves partly in Aramaic. Those preserved are of varying worth. Some elements clearly go back to a pre-Masoretic text, but as they have come down to us, most are the result of much later revisions. An exception should perhaps be made of the Palestinian Targum of the Pentateuch (MS. Neofiti I) discovered in 1957 in the Vatican library. This is said to be pre-Mishnaic.

The other important Targums are four in number. The first two together form what is known as the Babylonian Targum (not to be confused with the Babylonian Talmud—a vast commentary on things scriptural and traditional). This composite Targum was actually composed in Palestine (perhaps in the second century A.D.), but edited in Babylonia (in the third or even fifth century A.D.). Its first part—that on the Pentateuch—is known separately as the Targum of Onkelos. This man Onkelos is supposed to have been contemporary with Rabbi Akiba, but the name is now usually regarded as a misspelling of Aquila—the ultra-literal translator of the Old Testament into Greek. 'Onkelos' perhaps marks a stage in conforming an older Targum to Akiba's revised Hebrew text as adopted by Aquila. The second part of the Babylonian Targum is called the Targum of Jonathan, and it covers the Former and Latter Prophets. Kahle believes that 'Jonathan' here is merely a translation of 'Theodotion' and that this man was later identified with Jonathan ben Uzziel, a disciple of Rabbi Hillel (first century A.D.). This Targum was revised in Palestine before being rewritten in Babylonia. It paraphrases more than Onkelos. A critical edition of the Babylonian Targum has been edited by A. Sperber in four volumes (1959 ff.).

The third, the Jerusalem Targum, or Targum Yerushalmi, is a late periphrastic Targum. In the Pentateuch it is based possibly on Onkelos or, rather, his original. In the Prophets it is based on Jonathan, but only fragments of this portion survive. There exists also a different recension of the Pentateuch section, in which the abbreviated title 'T.J.' was misinterpreted 'Targum of Jonathan', so that it is now usually styled 'Pseudo-Jonathan' to distinguish it from the genuine Targum of Jonathan, which is on the Prophets, not the Pentateuch.

Here it is necessary to mention only one other Targum; this dealt with the Pentateuch. On account of its present state it is called the Fragment Targum, or Targum Yerushalmi II. The complexity of Targumic studies may be seen from Paul E. Kahle, *The Cairo Geniza*, second edition, pp. 191–208.

The Samaritan Pentateuch

This is not a translation, but a Hebrew text—of the Pentateuch alone—which has had a history separate from that of the M.T. since the time of the Samaritan schism. At what period the Samaritan and Jerusalem communities broke off relations with one another finally is not certain, but it was evidently after the time of Nehemiah's second visit to Jerusalem (432 B.C.), and before the virtual canonization of the Prophetical books of the Old Testament, *c.* 200 B.C. If we date the schism about the middle of the fourth century B.C., we may be not far out. About this time the Samaritan community built their rival temple on Mount Gerizim, and from then on their copy of the Hebrew Bible—which remained restricted to the Pentateuch, and written in the old Hebrew script—was copied independently of the Jewish tradition. There are some six thousand variations between the S.P. and the M.T., in which the S.P. agrees with the LXX some 1,900 times, so it is alleged. Most of the discrepancies are orthographic, e.g. the presence or absence of vowel letters; but occasionally there are serious differences which indicate wilful alterations in one or the other, e.g. in Deuteronomy xxvii. 4 the M.T. commands the tablets of the Law to be set up on Mount Ebal, whereas the S.P. reads Mount Gerizim (the site of their temple). Which is original is not certain, but probability leans to the side of the S.P. here. The S.P. was translated into Greek, Aramaic (the so-called 'Samaritan Version') and Arabic.

Minor Versions

All other early versions owe their origin to Christian hands, and were translated from the Greek. Such are the Sahidic, Akhmimic, Fayyumic, and Bohairic, which were all dialects of 'Coptic' (the Arabic form of the word 'Egyptian'). They were made between A.D. 359 and 650. In Ethiopia there is the Ethoipic version, translated in the fifth to sixth centuries, and later revised from the Arabic versions.

Had an early Arabic version been made from the Hebrew, it would have been valuable; but none is known before the seventh century A.D., and its only value apparent so far is for the Greek text. An Arabic version of Daniel is thought by H. S. Gehman to represent a better Hexaplaric text than any other witness (Pfeiffer, *Introduction to the Old Testament*, p. 118).

The Armenian Bible was made from the LXX in the fifth century, and was revised from the Syriac. The closely associated Georgian Bible is later, but preserves some earlier readings. The Slavonic (ninth century) and Gothic (*c.* 350) are now mere fragments.

Polyglot Bibles

Almost all the main Versions may be found printed side by side with the M.T. in Brian Walton's *Biblia*

Sacra Polyglotta (1657), which is more complete in this respect than the *Complutensian* (1514–17), the Antwerp *Biblia Regia* (1569–72), or the *Paris* (1629–45) Polyglots. A new Polyglot Bible is in preparation in Spain, and a photographic reprint of Walton's Polyglot is available.

Besides the books already mentioned, attention should be drawn to the convenient collection of material in *The Bible in its Ancient and English Versions*, ed. H. W. Robinson (1940), also B. J. Roberts, *The Old Testament Text and Versions* (1951), and F. G. Kenyon, *Our Bible and the Ancient Manuscripts* (revised by A. W. Adams, 1958).

5

THE TEXTUAL WORK OF THE MASORETES

A MASORETE was one who preserved and handed down 'masorah' (textual) *tradition*. No full account of the herculean labours of these 'transmitters of tradition' can be attempted, but a few of their contributions to the study of the text of the Old Testament may be mentioned. The Masoretes made numerous attempts to improve the text that they had received, as well as handing on earlier more drastic alterations, in a critical apparatus. Shorter annotations on peculiarities in the text were collected together on the margins of their codices, and are called the 'Masora Parva', to distinguish them from the longer rubrics called the 'Masora Magna', which were put at the beginning and end of their MSS.

Suggested or actual emendations were made by the Masoretes, not on the evidence of the ancient Versions, or of critical study, but on tradition, which was no doubt very much more complex and self-contradictory than appears at first sight now (cf. the conflicting expositions of rival Rabbis in the Mishna). The Hebrew text resulting from the labours of the Masoretes is that now read in all synagogues and printed in all Hebrew Bibles, and is known as the 'Masoretic Text', or M.T.

The Divisions in the Masoretic Text

The division of the separate books into *chapters* is first mentioned about A.D. 1330, and is thus late, and due, in fact, to Christian practice. The division into *verses* is much older, and goes back beyond A.D. 200 (Mishna). A verse in Hebrew is called a *Pasuq*. Verse division was finally fixed by ben Asher in the tenth century, when he divided the Pentateuch into 5,845 verses instead of 5,888 (Babylonian reckoning) or 15,842 (Palestinian reckoning). The purpose of the verse division is not certain; some suggest that it originated in the 'line' of poetry, others that it was the amount read out at a time to the Paraphraser (*Methurgeman*), who turned it into Aramaic for the synagogue congregation. Verses are marked off by two dots(:) called *Soph Pasuq* ('End of the Verse'), though this is first mentioned after A.D. 500.

The next division of the Hebrew text was into natural sense-paragraphs, later marked off by a letter *Pe* (for *Pethucha*, 'open'), if it was an 'open' paragraph, or by a letter *Samekh* (for *Sethuma*, 'closed'), if a 'closed' paragraph—these latter are usually the shorter.

The final division is that into liturgical sections. These are of two, mutually exclusive, forms, viz. *Sedarim* and *Perashiyoth*. The former, which are marked throughout the Bible by means of a letter *Samekh* in the margin, divided the Pentateuch into sufficient lessons for the Palestinian triennial cycle of reading; whereas the latter—indicated variously, by the letter *Pe* written three times in the text gap, or by writing

Parasha in full or in part in the margin—number fifty-four, for the finally dominant Babylonian annual cycle. The section from the Prophets to accompany a *Parasha* is called a *Haphtara*.

Special Features in the Masoretic Text

The oldest trace of textual criticism in the M.T. is thought by Ginsburg (pp. 318 ff.) to be the series of dots placed over certain doubtful words—ten in the Pentateuch, five in the remainder, e.g. Genesis xxxiii. 4, over 'and he kissed him'. Another way of drawing attention is the upright stroke (*Paseq*, 'Divider') after a word. Its original significance is not certain; the Masoretes seem to regard it as intended to keep two words apart. This may be its use in some cases, but in possibly earlier instances it seems intended to draw attention to a textual error not to be corrected (our '*sic!*'). There are about 480 occurrences of Paseq in the M.T., e.g. after 'and he arose' (Genesis xxxii. 23).

A letter *Nun* reversed is used nine times (ten with Genesis xi. 32), probably to indicate passages which are out of place, e.g. Numbers x. 35–6, which precede verse 34 in the LXX. In twenty-eight places a gap has been left in the text to indicate, at least in some of the cases, the loss of a word or phrase, e.g. the loss of Cain's speech after 'his brother' (Genesis iv. 8).

The first word of a book is begun with a larger letter; this also marks the middle letter of the Pentateuch (either Leviticus xiii. 33 or xi. 42), important passages (e.g. Exodus xxxiv. 7), and the like. Letters smaller than the usual occur in some words, e.g. a *He* in Genesis ii. 4. Raised, broken, or otherwise unusual letters mark other features of the text to which the Masoretes wished to direct attention for critical purposes, e.g. the raised *Nun* in Judges xviii. 30 which makes the name 'Moses' read 'Manasseh', out of reverence for the Lawgiver.

The most common text-critical feature of the M.T. is the *Qere* and *Kethib*, in which the faulty word (*Kethib*, 'written') is left in the text, but is now pointed with the vowels of the correct word (*Qere*, 'to be read'), whose consonants are written in the margin. This latter provision is not carried out with a 'perpetual *Qere*' such as 'Adonai' for 'Yahweh', owing to its frequence. Not only grammatically incorrect forms, but blasphemous or obscene expressions are thus treated also, e.g. the root שכב is always substituted for the coarse word שגל (Deuteronomy xxviii. 30, etc.).

When the scribes were not so convinced of the necessity of a *Qere*, they often appended a variant reading with the note *Sebir* ('supposed' to be the correct reading), but this is not to be substituted even in reading, e.g. the verb 'and he said' in 1 Samuel xii. 5 has the note, '*Sebir*: "and they said" '. It is not known whether a *Sebir* marks a conjectural or a textual variant. Occasionally what is called a *Sebir* by one school is regarded as a *Qere* by another, e.g. Isaiah xxx. 32, the *Kethib* 'with it' has an alternative 'with them' which is *Qere* ('to be read') according to one school, but is only *Sebir* ('supposed') according to another.

As shown elsewhere, the scribes did make alterations in the consonantal text for dogmatic and reverential reasons. Some of these are listed under official approval as *Tiqqune Hassopherim* ('corrections of the scribes'), e.g. Job xxxii. 3, 'They condemned *Job*' is said to have read originally, 'They condemned *God*'. Even these eighteen listed corrections (for the others, see Ginsberg, pp. 347 ff.) cannot be accepted by us without scrutiny —some are doubtful.

A less important scribal change is recorded among others in the Talmud (*Nedarim*, 37*b*–38*a*); it is the pointing—or, rather, pronunciation—*hā'āreṣ* instead of *hā'ereṣ* and the reading of the dual-type ending with *shāmayim* and *miṣrayim*.

It will be seen from what has been said that the Jews themselves were conscious of imperfections in the existing copies of the Scriptures; and scholars of many ages have attempted to ascertain the original text. Such early endeavours as have been indicated above touch only a small percentage of the passages corrupted by the vicissitudes of history. They still need to be supplemented by present-day critical and scientific study, using all the helps of better instruments and improved technique.

6

TYPES OF ERROR IN THE MASORETIC TEXT

There are two entirely distinct types of error in the Masoretic Text. The first (A) is due to the absence of vowels and word spaces from the original text, with consequent misinterpretation by the Masoretes; the second (B) is more extensive and arises from alterations of the original consonantal text.

(*A*) *Textual Misunderstanding*

Under this heading we may list three types of error:

I. Wrong pointing

Where only consonants are written, several possibilities exist in the way of pronunciation, and so meaning. The M.T. has not always chosen the correct one, e.g. in Isaiah vii. 11 the M.T. reads, 'Ask thee a sign from Yahweh thy God, going deep *ask* (שְׁאָלָה), or going up aloft', whereas, as the parallelism and some of the Versions show, we should read '. . . going deep *unto Sheol* (שְׁאֹלָה) . . .'.

II. Wrong word division

Hebrew, as already stated, was originally written

without appreciable spaces between words, and so the text has sometimes been divided wrongly, and pointed accordingly, e.g. in Amos vi. 12 the M.T. took 'Does one plough בבקרים?' to mean 'Does one plough with oxen?' (literally 'oxens'); since this gives the wrong answer, 'Yes', it is clear that the correct division is בַּבָּקָר יָם, 'Does one plough *the sea with oxen*?'

Occasionally one word may be divided into two. e.g. in Isaiah ii. 20 the M.T. has divided the word for 'to the moles' (לַחֲפַרְפָּרוֹת) into two. Often the letter *Waw* at the end of a verb is attached, instead, to the beginning of the next word, as if it were the conjunction 'and', e.g. in the middle of 1 Samuel xiv. 21.

III Wrong sentence division

In Joel ii. 1–2 it is clear from the metrical structure that the words כִּי קָרוֹב 'for it is near', are not an appendix to verse 1, but the beginning of verse 2: '*For* a day of darkness . . . *is near.*'

(*B*) *Textual Corruption*

Unlike the corrections listed above, the following types of error all need an alteration of the ccnsonantal text. The corruptions may be accidental or deliberate, but are best classed under three main heads as showing (I) alteration, (II) addition, (III) omission with regard to the original text.

I. Alteration

1. *Metathesis or transposition.* The former term is

usually reserved for the disarrangement of consonants within one word, the latter is of wider application.

(*a*) Sometimes it is a case of two consonants changing place in a word, e.g. in Psalm xlix. 12 the M.T. reads, 'Their *inward parts* (קִרְבָּם) are their houses for ever', where we should certainly transpose two consonants and read, 'Their *grave*(*s*) (קִבְרָם) are their houses for ever'.

(*b*) A clear instance of two nouns which have had their respective suffixes interchanged is to be found in Amos vi. 2, where the M.T. gives, 'Is *their* border wider than *your* border?' Since this would give the wrong answer, 'Yes', *your* must be read for *their*, and vice versa.

(*c*) Two whole words have been transposed in Nahum i. 6, where it is the second word, not the first, which begins with the letter *Zayin* needed for the acrostic.

(*d*) Occasionally whole verses have been transposed, e.g. in Nahum i. 9, where the *Lamedh* and *Mem* lines of the acrostic poem have been reversed in order. In Judges xvi, verse 24 ought to follow verse 25.

2. *Confusion.* This is of two types; which occurs, depends upon whether the scribe was writing from dictation or from sight.

(*a*) Auditory confusion substitutes one letter for another similar in sound, e.g. לא for לו (1 Samuel ii. 16; 1 Kings xi. 22, etc.) also אדני for יהוה, since the reader pronounced them both the same—the so-called *Qere perpetuum.*

(*b*) Visual confusion arises between letters similar in form, especially *Daleth* and *Resh*, e.g. in Isaiah xiv. 4 the M.T. reads, 'the *golden* city (מַדְהֵבָה) is at rest', but we should certainly follow the Greek and Syriac Versions in reading, 'the boisterous city (מַרְהֵבָה) is at rest'. The possibility of visual confusion having arisen in the *old* Hebrew script, as well as in the square script, must be borne in mind, particularly in the Pentateuch.

3. *Conjecture.* Conjectural emendation is not a discovery of recent times; where the fading of the ink or a tear or hole in the exemplar made the reading illegible, the scribe—if he had no other help—was reduced to one of two expedients: either omission or conjecture. In many cases the context would help the scribe to guess correctly, but even where it did not, it is difficult to detect it unless he made a bad blunder, or a different recension gives us the original uncorrupted, e.g. in 2 Samuel xxii. 33 illegibility apparently led the scribe to guess the line as 'God is *my refuge* (מָעוּזִּי), power', but the poetic parallelism, the renderings in the Versions, and, lastly and decisively, the duplicate of the verse in Psalm xviii. 32 make it clear that the original had: 'God *has girded me* (מְאַזְּרֵנִי) with power.' Mental wool-gathering on the part of the copyist no doubt accounts for some alterations.

4. *Dogmatic substitution.* There are some cases of the deliberate substitution of a different word so as not to offend the more highly developed sensibilities of later times, e.g. in Psalm liii we find the generic 'God' (אֱלֹהִים), whereas the other recension of the same poem,

Psalm xiv, kept the individual 'Yahweh' יהוה). In 1 Samuel xiv. 18 the M.T. reads, 'the ark of God'; it should be 'the Ephod', as in the LXX, but has been changed because the Ephod came to be considered idolatrous.

II. Addition

We now come to the second main sub-division, that in which the original text has been added to in one way or another, consciously or unconsciously, to give us our present M.T.

1. *Mechanical addition and dittography.* (*a*) Familiarity may lead a scribe subconsciously to add a letter to the word in his copy if it thereby forms a commoner word, e.g. in 2 Samuel xxii. 44 'Thou wilt keep me (תִּשְׁמְרֵנִי)' should read as in the duplicate Psalm xviii. 44, 'Thou wilt set me (תְּשִׂמֵנִי)', without the *Resh*. The scribe may even be led on by a word in his text to write down some common phrase or quotation which begins with the same word, e.g. in Psalm cxxxvii.7 the word *Yahweh* in 'Remember, Yahweh, . . .' is superfluous, and spoils the metre.

(*b*) A fairly frequent fault in copying is dittography, in which the scribe writes either a single letter, or even as much as a whole word twice instead of once, e.g. in Isaiah lxiii. 2 for the M.T. 'Why is *to thy garment* (לִלְבוּשֶׁךָ) red?' we should read, 'Why is *thy garment* (לְבוּשֶׁךָ) red?' In Ezekiel xlviii. 16 the Kethib '*five five* hundred' should be read '*five* hundred' simply, as the *Qere* itself shows by not pointing the second חמש.

2. *Comment.* Often a word is inserted into the text—frequently to the detriment of the original, or any, meaning—because a previous owner had written it on the margin of the MS., and a later copyist took it for an integral element of the text. Such additions may belong to any of four classes:

(*a*) Comment proper, e.g. in Hosea xiv. 9, 'Who is so wise that he may understand these things . . .?' can hardly be Hosea's own remark (cf. the reference to the difficulty of St. Paul's Epistles recorded in 2 Peter iii. 16).

(*b*) Glossing (from Latin *glossa*, an antiquated or difficult word). A gloss is a word of common occurrence used to explain a rare word in the text. 'Gloss' is, however, often used rather loosely of almost any marginal comment, e.g. in Zechariah vi. 3 the horses of the fourth chariot are described in the R.V. as 'grisled bay' (M.T., בְּרֻדִּים אֲמֻצִּים), but אֲמֻצִּים clearly means 'strong', and not a colour, and is almost certainly a gloss intended to explain the unusual word בְּרֻדִּים, which really means 'piebald', as we now know.

(*c*) Corrections. A mistake noticed by the scribe in the text is sometimes corrected in the margin, and later incorporated in the text along with the mistake, e.g. in 1 Samuel xviii. 10 the easiest explanation of the difficult phrase, 'An evil divine spirit' (רוּחַ אֱלֹהִים רָעָה), is that 'evil' was an improvement intended to take the place of 'divine', but that it has been added thereto; cf. also the ungrammatical addition of 'the covenant' (הַבְּרִית) after 'the ark' (הָאָרוֹן) in Joshua iii. 14.

(*d*) Variants. Sometimes two words or phrases which duplicate one another unnecessarily may be found in the text, and appear to represent alternatives —possibly the readings of two different MSS. then circulating, both with some authority, e.g. 1 Samuel xxviii. 3, 'and they buried him in Ramah and in his city' (וַיִּקְבְּרֻהוּ בְרָמָה וּבְעִירוֹ); here 'in his city' seems to be a variant of 'in Ramah'—the 'and' is lacking in the LXX and Vulgate.

3. *Conflation.* Conflation is a term best reserved for the more complicated type of variant which arises when two differing accounts of one incident or accounts of two similar incidents are blended together, e.g. Zechariah xii. 2, the M.T. 'and even upon Judah shall be in siege, upon Jerusalem' (וְגַם עַל־יְהוּדָה יִהְיֶה בַמָּצוֹר עַל־יְרוּשָׁלָםִ) seems to be a blend of two sets of alternatives, which make an impossible text as they stand. Sorting them out, we get the four possibilities: (i) 'And even upon Judah shall there be siege'; (ii) 'And even Judah shall be in siege'; (iii) and (iv) are the same as the above, with the substitution of 'Jerusalem' for 'Judah'.

4. *Interpolation.* An interpolation is a passage added to the original, but not combined with it, so that it can usually be taken out again without leaving an obvious gap, e.g. for the kings of Israel and Judah mentioned in 1 Kings xvi. 23 to 2 Kings i. 17 there are two parallel but inconsistent synchronisms, one in the M.T. and LXX, the other in Lucian's Greek. In 2 Kings i. 17 Lucian's synchronism has been inter-

polated into the M.T. (but not the LXX), saying that Jehoram of Israel commenced his reign in the second year of Jehoram of Judah; this is inconsistent with the real M.T. synchronism of 2 Kings iii. 1, which dates it in the eighteenth year of Jehoshaphat.

III. Omission

Under this head we include cases of all types in which the M.T. is shorter than the original text. These all seem to be unintentional, for the best of scribes is occasionally guilty of carelessness, and there are factors which make omission easier.

1. *Simple omission.* Single letters, whole words, even phrases, or complete verses may be lost either from the carelessness of the copyist, or because of some illegibility in his exemplar, e.g. in 2 Samuel xxii. 41 the meaningless תַּתָּה should be נָתַתָּה, 'thou hast given', as in the duplicate passage, Psalm xviii. 41. In Genesis iv. 8 the phrase, 'Let us go into the field' (נֵלְכָה הַשָּׂדֶה), as preserved in the older Versions, has dropped out of the M.T. after 'And Cain said unto his brother Abel'.

2. *Unresolved abbreviations.* The easiest way to explain some omissions is on the theory that, in some MSS., abbreviated forms existed for plurals and proper names, e.g. in 1 Samuel xx. 38 הַחִצִי must stand for הַחִצִּים; in Exodus viii. 23 'As He shall command us' (כַּאֲשֶׁר יֹאמַר אֵלֵינוּ) is rendered in the LXX 'As *Yahweh has* commanded us' (כַּאֲשֶׁר יהוה אָמַר אֵלֵינוּ). (We might also mention here the case of a wrongly resolved

abbreviation in 2 Chronicles xxi. 2 which describes Jehoshaphat as 'King of *Israel*' instead of 'King of *Judah*', probably because מֶלֶךְ י׳ which could stand for either, was wrongly expanded.)

3. *Homoiosis* ('similarity', i.e. the repetition of the same or similar letters or words.) It is a common phenomenon to find haplography ('half-writing', i.e. writing a letter or word once when it should occur twice); it may be regarded as the opposite of dittography. It is particularly common where the similarity is between the last consonants of two words, or the last words of two phrases, and in such cases is known as *homoioteleuton* ('similar end').

(*a*) Haplography of letters, e.g. in Genesis xxxii. 23 בַּלַּיְלָה הוּא stands for בַּלַּיְלָה הַהוּא, 'on that night'.

(*b*) Haplography of words, e.g. in Judges xx. 13 'And Benjamin were not willing' (וְלֹא אָבוּ בִּנְיָמִין) should read, 'And the Benjaminites were not willing' (וְלֹא אָבוּ בְּנֵי בִּנְיָמִין).

(*c*) Homoioteleuton on a large scale is found in the following example, where the M.T. omits the whole of phrase B owing to the scribe's eye passing from the *Israel* at the end of phrase A to the same word at the end of phrase B, whence he took up his copying at C, and we would have lost a whole sentence were it not for the LXX, Old Latin and Vulgate which have preserved it:

A. 'And Saul said unto Yahweh, God of *Israel*,

B. 'Why has thou not answered thy servant this day? If this iniquity is in me or in my son Jonathan, oh Yahweh, God of Israel, give Urim; but if this iniquity is in thy people *Israel*,

C. give Tummim. . . .' (1 Samuel xiv. 41).

The corruptions listed above as examples have almost all been 'simple', i.e. only one stage from the original. In many cases one corruption has led to further corruptions in the scribe's attempt to restore a meaning to his text. In such a case the text may easily go beyond all hope of repair. We may, however, to close this chapter, cite one fairly simple case of a compound corruption which can be traced back in two stages with the help of some of the Versions. In Judges xi. 20 occurs the phrase, 'And Sihon *did not trust* (וְלֹא הֶאֱמִין) Israel to cross his border', according to the M.T., but some Versions have 'And Sihon *refused* (וַיְמָאֵן) to allow (תֵּת) Israel to cross his border'. Disregarding the ultimate omission of 'to allow' from the M.T., either owing to homoioteleuton with the following אֶת־ or because it did not make sense, we have the following steps in the change of 'And he refused' (וַיְמָאֵן) into 'And he did not trust (וְלֹא־הֶאֱמִין). First, *metathesis* into וַיַּאֲמֵן, 'and he trusted'; second, *correction* of this by the insertion of the negative and consequent adjustment of the tense into וְלֹא־הֶאֱמִין.

For Further Reading

Some Notes on Titles Referred to in This Book, and Some Additional Suggestions

By D. R. Ap-Thomas:

"Absalom, Abishalom," "City," etc., in *Dictionary of the Bible,* ed. James Hastings, rev. ed. Frederick C. Grant and H. H. Rowley. New York: Scribner, 1963.

"Jerusalem," in *Archaeology and Old Testament Study,* ed. by D. Winton Thomas for the British Society for Old Testament Study (Oxford University Press, 1967).

"Two Notes on Isaiah," in *Essays in Honour of G. W. Thatcher,* ed. E. C. B. MacLaurin (Sydney University Press, 1966).

Translations (from German): O. Eissfeldt, "The Prophetic Literature," and W. Baumgartner, "The Wisdom Literature," in *The Old Testament and Modern Study,* ed. H. H. Rowley. Oxford: Clarendon, 1951. Pp. 115–61 and 210–37.

Translation (from German): Martin Noth. *The Laws in the Pentateuch and Other Essays* (Edinburgh: Oliver & Boyd, 1966).

Translation (from Norwegian): Sigmund Mowinckel. *The Psalms in Israel's Worship.* 2 vols. Oxford: Basil Blackwell, and Nashville: Abingdon, 1962.

Referred to in this Book:

Foreword

Ginsburg, Christian David. *Introduction to the Massoretico-critical edition of the Hebrew Bible.* London: Trinitarian Bible Society, 1897.

Eissfeldt, Otto. *Einleitung in das Alte Testament.* Tübingen: J. C. B. Mohr, 1934; 2nd ed., 1956; 3rd ed., 1964. English translation by P. R. Ackroyd, *The Old Testament: An Introduction.* Oxford: Blackwell, 1965.

Pfeiffer, Robert H. *Introduction to the Old Testament.* New York: Harper, 1941.

Chapter 1, "The Canon of the Old Testament"

Biblia Hebraica. RUDOLF KITTEL and PAUL KAHLE (eds.). 3rd ed., A. ALT and O. EISSFELDT (eds.). Stuttgart: Privilegierte Württembergische Bibelanstalt, 1937; 7th ed., 1963.

Septuaginta id est vetus testamentum graece iuxta LXX interpretes. ALFRED RAHLFS (ed.). 2 vols. Stuttgart: Privilegierte Württembergische Bibelanstalt, 1935.

Chapter 2, "Language, Script, and Writing Materials"

NOTH, MARTIN. *The History of Israel.* Rev. trans. P. R. Ackroyd. New York: Harper, 1960.

ALBRIGHT, W. F. *From the Stone Age to Christianity: Monotheism and the Historical Process.* Baltimore: Johns Hopkins Press, 1940; 2nd ed., 1957.

DRIVER, S. R. *Notes on the Hebrew Text of the Books of Samuel.* 2nd rev. ed. Oxford: Clarendon, 1913.

GESENIUS-KAUTZSCH. Gesenius' *Hebrew Grammar* as edited and enlarged by the late E. KAUTZSCH. 2nd English ed. rev. A. E. Cowley. Oxford: Clarendon, 1910; reprinted with corrections, 1949.

DIRINGER, DAVID. *The Story of the Aleph Beth.* New York: Thomas Yoseloff, 1960.

THOMAS, D. WINTON (ed.). *Documents from Old Testament Times.* New York: Nelson, 1958.

KENYON, FREDERIC. *Books and Readers in ancient Greece and Rome.* 2nd ed. Oxford: Clarendon, 1951.

Chapter 3, "Vocalization and Standardization of the Text"

SPERBER, ALEXANDER. "Hebrew Based upon Greek and Latin Transliterations," *Hebrew Union College Annual* (Cincinnati), 12–13 (1937–38), 103–274.

BURROWS, MILLAR. *More Light on the Dead Sea Scrolls.* New York: Viking, 1958.

KENYON, FREDERIC. *The Story of the Bible.* New York: Dutton, 1937.

Chapter 4, "The Ancient Versions"

CHARLES, R. H. (ed.). *The Apocrypha and Pseudepigrapha of the Old Testament in English.* 2 vols. Oxford: Clarendon, 1913; reprinted 1963.

FIELD, FREDERIC. *Origenis Hexaplorum quae Supersunt.* 2 vols. Oxford, 1875; reprinted Hildesheim: G. Olms, 1964.

SWETE, HENRY BARCLAY. *The Old Testament in Greek according to the Septuagint.* Cambridge University Press, 1st ed., 1887 ff.; 4th ed., 1909 ff.

——. *Introduction to the Old Testament in Greek.* Cambridge University Press, 1st ed. 1900; 2nd rev. ed. by R. R. OTTLEY, 1914.

"The Cambridge Septuagint" = *The Old Testament in Greek,* ed. A. E. BROOKE and N. MCLEAN. Cambridge University Press, 1906 ff. (not completed).

"Göttingen Septuagint" = *Septuaginta Vetus Testamentum Graecum auctoritate Societatis Litterarum Gottingensis editum,* ed. A. RAHLFS, J. ZIEGLER, and others. Göttingen: Vandenhoeck & Ruprecht, 1926 ff. (in process).

KAHLE, PAUL E. *The Cairo Geniza.* ("Schweich Lectures for 1941.") London: Published for the British Academy by Oxford University Press, 1947; 2nd ed., New York: Praeger, 1960.

ROBINSON, H. WHEELER (ed.). *The Bible in its Ancient and English Versions.* Oxford: Clarendon, 1940.

ROBERTS, BLEDDYN J. *The Old Testament Text and Versions.* Cardiff: University of Wales Press, 1951.

KENYON, FREDERIC. *Our Bible and the Ancient Manuscripts,* rev. by A. W. ADAMS. New York: Harper, 1958.

ADDITIONAL TITLES:

A very detailed bibliography, as of 1951, is provided in B. J. ROBERTS, *The Old Testament Text and Versions* (noted above under chapter 4), pp. 286–314.

WÜRTHWEIN, ERNST. *The Text of the Old Testament: An Introduction to Kittel-Kahle's Biblia Hebraica,* trans. P. R. ACKROYD. Oxford: Basil Blackwell, 1957. A standard companion to the standard critical Hebrew Old Testament text, covering in much greater detail most topics treated in this Facet Book. Includes 41 plates of illustrations. A most helpful volume for the student past the "primer" stage, but the criticisms ought to be noted which were voiced by HARRY M. ORLINSKY in his review in the *Journal of Semitic Studies* 4, 2 (April, 1959), 149–51.

Survey articles on Old Testament text and versions are found in most Bible dictionaries. See especially the following reference works:

The Interpreter's Bible (New York and Nashville: Abingdon-Cokesbury). A. JEFFERY, "Text and Ancient Versions of the Old Testament," 1 (1952), 46–62; and J. C. TREVER, "Illustrated History of the Biblical Text," 12 (1957), 628–44.

The Interpreter's Dictionary of the Bible (New York and Nashville: Abingdon, 1962). B. J. ROBERTS, "Text, Old Testament," 4, 580–94; and B. M. METZGER, "Versions, Ancient," 4, 749–60.

Peake's Commentary on the Bible. New ed. MATTHEW BLACK and H. H. ROWLEY (New York: Nelson, 1962). B. J. ROBERTS, "Canon and Text of the Old Testament," pp. 73–80, and "The Ancient Versions of the Old Testament," pp. 81–85.

Hastings' *Dictionary of the Bible* (cited above, p. 51). H. S. GEHMAN, "Text and Versions of the Old Testament," pp. 972–79, and "Greek Versions of the Old Testament," pp. 347–54; H. F. D. SPARKS, "Vulgate," pp. 1025–28.

A Companion to the Bible. 2nd ed. H. H. ROWLEY (Edinburgh: T. & T. Clark, 1964). B. J. ROBERTS, "The Transmission of the Text" (Old Testament), pp. 144–62.

On Qumran finds and their textual significance, see especially:

CROSS, FRANK MOORE, JR. *The Ancient Library of Qumran and Modern Biblical Studies.* Rev. ed. Garden City: Doubleday Anchor Books, 1961. A similar survey appears in his article in *The Interpreter's Bible,* 12 (1957), 645–57.

——. "The History of the Biblical Text in the Light of Discoveries in the Judaean Desert," *Harvard Theological Review,* 57 (1964), 281-99.

For students beginning to read the Hebrew Old Testament, convenient linguistic and textual notes on certain of the biblical books are found in the series "Texts for Students" (London: S.P.C.K.) and in Norman Snaith's "Study Notes on Bible Books" (London: Epworth Press), as well as in G. J. Spurrell's old *Notes on the Text of the Book of Genesis* (Oxford: Clarendon, 1896).

For those who use the Kittel-Kahle *Biblia Hebraica,* "An English Key" to its symbols and Latin words and abbreviations has been prepared by Prescott H. Williams, Jr., of Austin (Texas) Presbyterian Theological Seminary; it is printed by the Bibelanstalt in Stuttgart and is now available with the Kittel text.

Facet Books Already Published

Biblical Series:

1. *The Significance of the Bible for the Church* by Anders Nygren (translated by Carl Rasmussen). 1963
2. *The Sermon on the Mount* by Joachim Jeremias (translated by Norman Perrin). 1963
3. *The Old Testament in the New* by C. H. Dodd. 1963
4. *The Literary Impact of the Authorized Version* by C. S. Lewis. 1963
5. *The Meaning of Hope* by C. F. D. Moule. 1963
6. *Biblical Problems and Biblical Preaching* by C. K. Barrett. 1964
7. *The Genesis Accounts of Creation* by Claus Westermann (translated by Norman E. Wagner). 1964
8. *The Lord's Prayer* by Joachim Jeremias (translated by John Reumann). 1964
9. *Only to the House of Israel? Jesus and the Non-Jews* by T. W. Manson. 1964
10. *Jesus and the Wilderness Community at Qumran* by Ethelbert Stauffer (translated by Hans Spalteholz). 1964
11. *Corporate Personality in Ancient Israel* by H. Wheeler Robinson. 1964
12. *The Sacrifice of Christ* by C. F. D. Moule. 1964
13. *The Problem of the Historical Jesus* by Joachim Jeremias (translated by Norman Perrin). 1964
14. *A Primer of Old Testament Text Criticism* by D. R. Ap-Thomas. 1966
15. *The Bible and the Role of Women* by Krister Stendahl (translated by Emilie Sander). 1966

Social Ethics Series:

1. *Our Calling* by Einar Billing (translated by Conrad Bergendoff). 1965
2. *The World Situation* by Paul Tillich. 1965

3. *Politics as a Vocation*
by Max Weber (translated by H. H. Gerth and C. Wright Mills). 1965
4. *Christianity in a Divided Europe*
by Hanns Lilje. 1965
5. *The Bible and Social Ethics* by Hendrik Kraemer. 1965
6. *Christ and the New Humanity* by C. H. Dodd. 1965
7. *What Christians Stand For in the Secular World*
by William Temple. 1965
8. *Legal Responsibility and Moral Responsibility*
by Walter Moberly. 1965
9. *The Divine Command: A New Perspective on Law and Gospel* by Paul Althaus (translated by Franklin Sherman). 1966
10. *The Road to Peace*
by John C. Bennett, Kenneth Johnstone, C. F. von Weizsäcker, Michael Wright. 1966
11. *The Idea of a Natural Order: With an Essay on Modern Asceticism* by V. A. Demant. 1966
12. *Kerygma, Eschatology, and Social Ethics*
by Amos Niven Wilder. 1966
13. *Affluence and the Christian*
by Hendrik Van Oyen. 1966
14. *Luther's Doctrine of the Two Kingdoms*
by Heinrich Bornkamm (translated by Karl H. Hertz). 1966

Historical Series:

1. *Were Ancient Heresies Disguised Social Movements?*
by A. H. M. Jones. 1966
2. *Popular Christianity and the Early Theologians*
by H. J. Carpenter. 1966
3. *Tithing in the Early Church*
by Lukas Vischer (translated by Robert W. Schultz). 1966
4. *Jerusalem and Rome* by Hans von Campenhausen and Henry Chadwick. 1966

Body, **11 on 13 Baskerville**
Display, **Baskerville**
Paper: **White Spring Grove E.F.**

Ap-Thomas, Dafydd Rhys.
A primer of Old
Testament text criticism.

25,884

DATE	ISSUED TO
MAY 11 '67	J. Brauer
OCT 14 '68	Chris Heuer Ward
FEB 23 1982	N. Haas 182
OCT 17 1989	DAVID KATCHER

FACET fb BOOKS

brief, brilliant treatments of vital aspects of faith and life by leading authorities in the church today

BIBLICAL SERIES

edited by

John Reumann

Dr. Reumann, professor at the Lutheran Theological Seminary, Philadelphia, is also New Testament book review editor of the JOURNAL OF BIBLICAL LITERATURE.

A PRIMER OF OLD TESTAMENT TEXT CRITICISM

by D. R. Ap-Thomas

The aim of this book, writes the editor, is "to provide a primer or first introduction for students who are just learning Hebrew and for laymen who, even though they are without any introduction to the Hebrew language, want to know something about the text of the Old Testament." The following subjects are treated: the canon of the Old Testament; language, script, and writing material; vocalization and standardization of the text; the ancient versions; the textual work of the Masoretes; types of error in the Masoretic text. The author is Senior Lecturer in Hebrew and Biblical Studies in University College, Bangor, Wales.

For other titles in this series see last page

Cover art by Andrew A. Snyder

FORTRESS PRESS

PHILADELPHIA, PA. 19129